UNPLUG

BREATHE

CREATE

I0522066

A MONTH OF ATTRACTING CREATIVE INSPIRATION THROUGH MEDITATION

Unplug Breathe Create: A Month of Attracting Creative Inspiration Through Meditation is a work of my own creation.

The information in this book was correct at the time of publication, and the Author does not assume any liability for loss or damage caused by errors or omissions, again, this is my perspective, opinion, and experience, so it has been written as such.

Copyright © 2023 by megs thompson

All rights reserved.

No part of this book may be reproduced or transmitted in any form or by any means, electronic or mechanical, including photocopying, recording, or by any information and retrieval systems, without the written permission of the Publisher, except where permitted by law.

ISBN - 979-8-9875738-6-0

Cover, Book Design, and Layout by megs thompson, megswrites llc
www.megswrites.com

in omnia paratus publishing

www.inomniaparatuspublishing.com

"IMAGINATION IS
EVERYTHING. IT IS
THE PREVIEW OF
LIFE'S COMING
ATTRACTIONS."

—ALBERT EINSTEIN

This journal is part of the
UNPLUG BREATHE CREATE
series & designed to be used
alongside a bespoke guided
meditation.

Download this month's meditation
using the QR code below:

HOW TO BEST USE THIS JOURNAL & MEDITATION

UNPLUG

The first step to reconnecting with ourselves as creative beings is to unplug & disconnect even temporarily from the countless electronic tethers that keep us firmly held in the world of shoulds & must's.

BREATHE

Take a few deep breaths, paying close attention to the way oxygen moves through your mouth & nose, filling your lungs & reawakening the creative genius locked safely within you, exhaling any fears, hesitations, or doubts that may filter your magic.

CREATE

Release your desire to control, plan & perfect every step & movement you make. Embrace the often wild, messy & chaotic magic that comes with allowing your inner creative to explore & play. Prepare yourself to experience fulfillment & satisfaction in new & creative ways.

DAILY ROUTINE

While moving through your day, begin implementing the use of affirmations. Both habits & beliefs are formed & strengthened through consistent repetition & before you know it your thoughts will become truths.

Included below are powerful affirmations that when paired with your daily tasks & activities, will empower you through this month of finding & claiming your own creative space.

I recommend repeating one or more of these affirmations aloud anytime you find yourself in front of a mirror, washing your hands, or refilling your beverage of choice.

I ATTRACT CREATIVE INSPIRATION INTO MY LIFE WITH EASE.

I AM A POWERFUL, NATURALLY CREATIVE BEING.

I TAKE INSPIRED ACTION TOWARD MY UNIQUE CREATIVE GOALS.

30-DAY ENERGY TRACKER

When you've completed your daily meditation, make note of a single word or phrase that best describes your energy level in that moment.

Day 1	Day 2	Day 3	Day 4	Day 5
Day 6	Day 7	Day 8	Day 9	Day 10
Day 11	Day 12	Day 13	Day 14	Day 15
Day 16	Day 17	Day 18	Day 19	Day 20
Day 21	Day 22	Day 23	Day 24	Day 25
Day 26	Day 27	Day 28	Day 29	Day 30

DAY 1

During the meditation you visited your own unique creative sanctuary space. Describe that space here in as much detail as possible. What does it look like? How does it smell? Where's this space located? How do you feel when you're within your creative sanctuary?

_____

_____

_____

_____

_____

_____

_____

_____

_____

_____

_____

_____

_____

_____

ON A SCALE OF 1-5 WHAT'S YOUR
CURRENT CREATIVITY LEVEL?

DAY 2

Reflecting on the meditation, what negative thoughts, assumptions, beliefs & lies appeared on the screen within your creative sanctuary space? Don't spend too much time on this exercise. It's important to face these but not to focus your energy on them.

_____

_____

_____

_____

_____

_____

_____

_____

_____

_____

_____

_____

_____

_____

_____

_____

_____

_____

ON A SCALE OF 1-5 WHAT'S YOUR
CURRENT CREATIVITY LEVEL?

DAY 3

Now, let's focus on those big dreams, wishes, hopes & intentions that filled the screen within your mediation. Describe just one of those here, in as much detail as possible. How does this experience make you feel?

....

....

....

_____

_____

....

....

....

_____

_____

....

_____

_____

....

....

ON A SCALE OF 1-5 WHAT'S YOUR
CURRENT CREATIVITY LEVEL?

DAY 4

Revisiting your journal entry from yesterday, what is one inspired action that you can take towards attracting this dream & manifesting it into reality?

_____

_____

_____

_____

_____

_____

_____

_____

_____

_____

_____

_____

_____

_____

_____

_____

ON A SCALE OF 1-5 WHAT'S YOUR
CURRENT CREATIVITY LEVEL?

DAY 5

Let's dig into another of those big dreams, wishes, hopes & intentions that filled the screen within your mediation. Describe just one of those here, in as much detail as possible. How does this experience make you feel?

_____

_____

_____

_____

_____

_____

_____

_____

_____

_____

_____

_____

_____

_____

_____

ON A SCALE OF 1-5 WHAT'S YOUR
CURRENT CREATIVITY LEVEL?

DAY 6

Revisiting your journal entry from yesterday, what is one inspired action that you can take towards attracting this dream & manifesting it into reality?

_____

_____

_____

_____

_____

_____

_____

_____

_____

_____

_____

_____

_____

_____

_____

_____

ON A SCALE OF 1-5 WHAT'S YOUR
CURRENT CREATIVITY LEVEL?

DAY 7

Let's dig into another of those big dreams, wishes, hopes & intentions that filled the screen within your mediation. Describe just one of those here, in as much detail as possible. How does this experience make you feel?

_____

_____

_____

_____

_____

_____

_____

_____

_____

_____

_____

_____

_____

_____

ON A SCALE OF 1-5 WHAT'S YOUR
CURRENT CREATIVITY LEVEL?

DAY 8

Revisiting your journal entry from yesterday, what is one inspired action that you can take towards attracting this dream & manifesting it into reality?

ON A SCALE OF 1-5 WHAT'S YOUR
CURRENT CREATIVITY LEVEL?

DAY 9

Let's dig into another of those big dreams, wishes, hopes & intentions that filled the screen within your mediation. Describe just one of those here, in as much detail as possible. How does this experience make you feel?

_____

_____

_____

_____

_____

_____

_____

_____

_____

_____

_____

_____

_____

_____

ON A SCALE OF 1-5 WHAT'S YOUR
CURRENT CREATIVITY LEVEL?

DAY 10

Revisiting your journal entry from yesterday, what is one inspired action that you can take towards attracting this dream & manifesting it into reality?

_____

....

....

....

_____

_____

....

....

....

_____

_____

....

....

....

_____

_____

....

....

ON A SCALE OF 1-5 WHAT'S YOUR
CURRENT CREATIVITY LEVEL?

DAY 11

Let's dig into another of those big dreams, wishes, hopes & intentions that filled the screen within your mediation. Describe just one of those here, in as much detail as possible. How does this experience make you feel?

_____

_____

_____

_____

_____

_____

_____

_____

_____

_____

_____

_____

_____

_____

_____

_____

(decorative lotus illustration)

_____
_____
_____
_____
_____
_____
_____
_____
_____
_____
_____
_____
_____
_____
_____
_____

ON A SCALE OF 1-5 WHAT'S YOUR CURRENT CREATIVITY LEVEL?

DAY 12

Revisiting your journal entry from yesterday, what is one inspired action that you can take towards attracting this dream & manifesting it into reality?

ON A SCALE OF 1-5 WHAT'S YOUR
CURRENT CREATIVITY LEVEL?

DAY 13

Let's dig into one more of those big dreams, wishes, hopes & intentions that filled the screen within your mediation. Describe just one of those here, in as much detail as possible. How does this experience make you feel?

ON A SCALE OF 1-5 WHAT'S YOUR
CURRENT CREATIVITY LEVEL?

DAY 14

Revisiting your journal entry from yesterday, what is one inspired action that you can take towards attracting this dream & manifesting it into reality?

_____

_____

_____

_____

_____

_____

_____

_____

_____

_____

_____

_____

_____

_____

....

....

....

_____

_____

....

....

....

_____

_____

....

....

....

_____

_____

....

....

....

_____

ON A SCALE OF 1-5 WHAT'S YOUR CURRENT CREATIVITY LEVEL?

DAY 15

During the meditation you snapped a mental picture, capturing the moment you recognized that all of your dreams & desires are possible. Describe that image in as much detail as possible. How does this moment make you feel?

ON A SCALE OF 1-5 WHAT'S YOUR
CURRENT CREATIVITY LEVEL?

DAY 16

Inspired action comes in many different forms. One of those is by better connecting with your inner guidance system (IGS). It can sometimes seem like we're missing all of the 'hits' our IGS is giving us, so today, make a point of journaling or listing out the nudges, intuitive hunches, flashes of inspiration & ah-ha moments that you receive throughout the day. These can often hold clues as to the specific inspired action your higher-self is waiting for you to take.

ON A SCALE OF 1-5 WHAT'S YOUR
CURRENT CREATIVITY LEVEL?

DAY 17

Inspired action comes in many different forms. One of those is to take action NOW, as soon as you experience an inspiring idea. The longer we put off these sparks of genius, the more likely we are to allow our logical mind to suck all energy & excitement from that once brilliant idea. Leading to no action being taken at all. Not every idea we receive is going to be a great one, but the more often we're able to lean into & trust the nudges we receive, the more confidence we foster in our own innate knowing. When was the last time you took action without hesitation? How did the experience turn out? How much do you trust yourself to do so again in the future?

ON A SCALE OF 1-5 WHAT'S YOUR
CURRENT CREATIVITY LEVEL?

DAY 18

Occasionally, we each experience a lull in our creative inspiration. Worry not friend, this doesn't mean there's anything wrong with you or your inner creative genius. During these 'dry spells' it can be tempting to remain in place, taking no action at all, waiting & waiting & waiting for inspiration to strike. However, nothing changes if nothing changes & sometimes we need to give our creative inspiration a nudge. One method of kickstarting your creativity is to reconnect with you 'why.' Ask yourself, what are the reasons behind my following the path I am? What impact am I seeking to make on the world? What are the long term benefits of the life/business you're building?

<hr />
<hr />
<hr />
<hr />
<hr />
<hr />
<hr />
<hr />
<hr />
<hr />
<hr />
<hr />
<hr />
<hr />
<hr />

ON A SCALE OF 1-5 WHAT'S YOUR CURRENT CREATIVITY LEVEL?

DAY 19

Another method of kickstarting your creativity is to take a break. I know, it sounds counterintuitive, however you may be experiencing burn out & pushing yourself to be creative is only going to make things worse. Ask yourself, what are some ways that I can unplug, relax & recover? What places make you feel most relaxed? What activities or experiences allow you to unplug? Personally, I enjoy going outside, getting lost in the woods & being out of cell-phone coverage in order to reconnect with me. Use the space below to journal on a few different ideas to use in cases of your own burn out.

_____

_____

_____

_____

_____

_____

_____

_____

_____

_____

_____

ON A SCALE OF 1-5 WHAT'S YOUR
CURRENT CREATIVITY LEVEL?

DAY 20

Yet another method of kickstarting your own creativity is to allow yourself to consume the creative content of others. For some this means reading an inspirational book, watching uplifting videos, participating in a group meditation, or strolling through a gallery. What are your favorites ways to consume creative content? How can you go about making this a regular part of your daily routine?

ON A SCALE OF 1-5 WHAT'S YOUR
CURRENT CREATIVITY LEVEL?

DAY 21

What is one task that you complete every day. This may be something mundane, administrative & without much sparkle. How can you approach this task from a more creative standpoint?

....
....
....
....
....
_____
....
....
....
....
....
_____
....
....
....
....
....

ON A SCALE OF 1-5 WHAT'S YOUR
CURRENT CREATIVITY LEVEL?

DAY 23

Today, we're doing things a little different. Find a quiet space where you can comfortably be alone without distractions or interruptions for a few minutes. Gather 2 cups/glasses & fill one with water.

Once you've settled into a seated position, hold the glass of water in both hands, close your eyes & allow yourself to explore your feelings about your current situation. Your life right now, in this moment.

Once you've done this. Set down the glass of water & pick up the empty glass. Holding it in both hands, close your eyes & allow yourself to visualize & explore your feelings of the future. Of having achieved & experienced everything you desire.

While holding firm to this feeling, pour the water from your present situation into the glass representing your future. And, when you're ready, drink this now energetically invigorated water.

How did this exercise make you feel? What feelings did you experience as it relates to your current situation? What feelings did you experience as it relates to your future?

_____

....

....

ON A SCALE OF 1-5 WHAT'S YOUR
CURRENT CREATIVITY LEVEL?

DAY 24

When do you feel most in flow or aligned? Where in your body do you feel this? How would you describe this feeling or sensation? How might you be able to creatively amplify this feeling?

ON A SCALE OF 1-5 WHAT'S YOUR
CURRENT CREATIVITY LEVEL?

DAY 25

We're all familiar with the idea of creating a vision board at the beginning of the year, for the accomplishments & adventures we desire to experience over the course of the next 12 months. However, many people overlook the idea of creating a vision board for the specific life they wish to manifest into reality. Journal below what images you'd include on your own dream life vision board. And, if you feel so inclined, schedule time for yourself within the next few days to create this board & hang it somewhere you'll see it at the start & end of every day.

_____

_____

_____

_____

_____

_____

_____

_____

_____

_____

_____

ON A SCALE OF 1-5 WHAT'S YOUR
CURRENT CREATIVITY LEVEL?

DAY 26

As you've probably noticed, mindset is an integral piece of unlocking creative inspiration & a dream life. One practice that can help reset even the darkest of days, is to spend a few moments journaling about the things you're grateful in this moment. Using the space below, take a few moments to journal on what it is you're grateful for right now.

_____

_____

_____

_____

_____

_____

_____

_____

_____

_____

_____

_____

ON A SCALE OF 1-5 WHAT'S YOUR
CURRENT CREATIVITY LEVEL?

DAY 27

What lights you up? What topics or areas in life are you most passionate about? How do you currently use your creativity in these areas?

_____

_____

_____

_____

_____

_____

_____

_____

_____

_____

_____

_____

_____

_____

_____

_____

_____

ON A SCALE OF 1-5 WHAT'S YOUR
CURRENT CREATIVITY LEVEL?

DAY 28

Reflect on a recent accomplishment or achievement. Was the success of this endeavor something that you were confident in prior to completion? Did you feel or know that you were going to be successful? How might you be able to better trust those innate instincts in the future to reduce unnecessary worry or a desire to 'play small?'

ON A SCALE OF 1-5 WHAT'S YOUR
CURRENT CREATIVITY LEVEL?

DAY 29

When do you feel most empowered & confident? In what situations? With what people? In what tasks or environments? How can you better trust yourself & bring those feelings of empowerment & confidence into other areas of your life?

_____

_____

_____

_____

_____

_____

_____

_____

_____

_____

_____

_____

_____

_____

_____

_____

ON A SCALE OF 1-5 WHAT'S YOUR
CURRENT CREATIVITY LEVEL?

DAY 30

In order to continually grow & give ourselves the best chances of manifesting our dream lives, the most important thing we can do is to reflect & learn from our past actions & experiences. How might you be able to practice this cycle of reflecting & refining your dream life, expectations & inspired actions for a greater impact?

ON A SCALE OF 1-5 WHAT'S YOUR
CURRENT CREATIVITY LEVEL?

If you already have an
UNPLUG BREATHE CREATE
subscription, keep an eye on your
mailbox for your next delivery.

If you aren't yet a member but
would like to be, or are
interested in gifting a
membership to someone else,
scan the QR code below.

www.ingramcontent.com/pod-product-compliance
Lightning Source LLC
Chambersburg PA
CBHW070449130626
46553CB00006B/2326